Gods of Creation
IN WORLD MYTHOLOGY

Don Nardo

ReferencePoint
Press

San Diego, CA

About the Author

Classical historian and award-winning author Don Nardo has written numerous acclaimed volumes about ancient civilizations and peoples. They include more than three dozen overviews of the mythologies of the Sumerians, Babylonians, Egyptians, Greeks, Romans, Persians, Celts, Norse, Native Americans, and others. Nardo, who also composes and arranges orchestral music, lives with his wife, Christine, in Massachusetts.

© 2023 ReferencePoint Press, Inc.
Printed in the United States

For more information, contact:
ReferencePoint Press, Inc.
PO Box 27779
San Diego, CA 92198
www.ReferencePointPress.com

Picture Credits:
Cover: ZU_09/iStock

6: © Brooklyn Museum of Art/Bridgeman Images
9: © Isadora/Bridgeman Images
15: Fototeca Gilardi/Bridgeman Images
17: Sylvain Colett/Bridgeman
21: © Look and Learn/Bridgeman Images
24: © Look and Learn/Bridgeman Images
27: © Look and Learn/Bridgeman Images

31: De Agostini Picture Library Universal Images Group/Newscom
34: Shutterstock
39: Bridgeman Images
41: © Look and Learn/Bridgeman Images
45: Pictures from History/Bridgeman Images
48: Shutterstock
52: Bridgeman Images
55: AIWire/Newscom

LIBRARY OF CONGRESS CATALOGING-IN-PUBLICATION DATA

Names: Nardo, Don, 1947- author.
Title: Gods of creation in world mythology / by Don Nardo.
Description: San Diego, CA : ReferencePoint Press, 2021. | Series: Mythology around the world | Includes bibliographical references and index.
Identifiers: LCCN 2021036486 (print) | LCCN 2021036487 (ebook) | ISBN 9781678202644 (library binding) | ISBN 9781678202651 (ebook)
Subjects: LCSH: Creation--Mythology. | Gods.
Classification: LCC BL325.C7 N37 2021 (print) | LCC BL325.C7 (ebook) | DDC 202/.4--dc23
LC record available at https://lccn.loc.gov/2021036486
LC ebook record available at https://lccn.loc.gov/2021036487

CONTENTS

From the Dark Depths: A Burst of Light

In the spot now occupied by Egypt's capital, Cairo, thousands of years ago there stood the so-called City of the Sun, Iunu, better known in later ancient centuries by its Greek name—Heliopolis. In one of ancient Egypt's four principal creation tales, Iunu occupied the exact center of the world. In that once well-known and sacred story, the glorious god Atum entered existence suddenly, in a vivid burst of brilliant light, from the dark, mysterious depths of a primeval ocean that predated the earth itself. In fact, at that point even heaven did not yet exist, according to an ancient hymn to Atum. That holy writing depicted the god himself as saying, "The earth had not come into being, the creatures of the earth and the reptiles had not been made in that place. I lifted myself from the watery mass [and at first] I did not find a place where I could stand. I was alone. I took courage in my heart. I laid a foundation."[1]

The Egyptians called the foundation created by Atum the *benben*; it was the world's first scrap of dry land. The priests who maintained the shrines at Heliopolis claimed that the *benben* occupied the very center of the universe. Moreover, they asserted, though most of the sacred mound had long ago eroded away, a tiny piece of it still survived. Carefully guarded night and day, it rested in an inner chamber of Atum's temple at Heliopolis.

Atum

An ancient Egyptian creator god who was said to have fashioned the world's first piece of dry land

When the *benben* was still new, the story went, Atum stood on it as he began creating living things. At first, he made more gods, each of whom proceeded to fashion still more divine beings. Among the first whom Atum made were Shu, the deity of air, and his twin sister, Tefnut, goddess of moisture. Those two then brought forth two more gods—Geb, the embodiment of the earth itself, and his close companion, the sky goddess Nut. The Heliopolitan creation tale also told how the early gods fashioned the world's physical features, including the mountains, valleys, forests, and seas. Then came humanity. "Men and women arose from tears which came forth from my eye,"[2] Atum was depicted as uttering in another sacred writing. Finally, the Egyptians believed, the mighty creator made the many kinds of plants and animals found in nature.

Shu

The Egyptian deity of air, who in turn created other gods

A Basic Question of Origins

Despite what the early Egyptians thought, Atum's story is far from unique. The fact is that throughout history all human cultures had creation stories in which one or more gods arose, often in a burst of light, from the dark depths of nonexistence. That divine being then progressed to one or more acts of creation. This idea of a miraculous creation by one or multiple thinking beings is one of a few core cultural concepts—also including love, death, and war— that have long been universal to human societies. In the words of the late, noted American anthropologist Robert Carneiro:

Among the most basic questions raised by human beings are those of *origins*. How did the human species arise? How

5

was the earth created? What about the sun? the moon? the stars? Why do we have night and day? Why do people die? No human society lacks answers to such questions. While these answers vary greatly in detail, they are, for primitive peoples as a whole, similar in their basic form: people and the world exist because they were brought into being by a series of creative acts. Moreover, this creation is usually regarded as the work of supernatural beings or forces.[3]

Those beings or forces are of course the creator gods of the diverse human mythologies. Today, perhaps the most obvious trait they have in common is that they appear in entertaining tales

According to ancient Egyptian lore, the sky goddess Nut, pictured here, was one of the first of many deities fashioned by the potent creator god Atum.

of colorful times and places that no longer exist. But there is an equally important factor that those deities and their stories share. Namely, to the ancient peoples who worshipped those gods, their creation tales had the ring of truth and were relevant to everyday life.

In part this was because ancient societies had little or no sense of history or progress. They did not conceive of human culture becoming progressively more advanced over time. As the late historian H.W.F. Saggs put it, they assumed the world had changed little or not at all since a god or gods had created it in the distant past. "With no concept of social progress," he wrote, "they had no incentive to make a conscious record of life in the thousands of years before [their own time]."[4]

This explains why the early Hindus, Babylonians, Egyptians, and other ancients did not pen formal histories to record ongoing events for the benefit of future generations. Instead, they tended to fall back on their collected myths. And always central to those tales were the ones that told how the gods, world, and people originally came to be.

CHAPTER ONE

The Creation According to the Greeks

Armies surged across the earth's scorched surface, as their combatants—magnificent beings taller than houses—hurled trees, giant boulders, and lightning bolts at one another. Leading the first army in that savage battle was Cronos, the dim-witted but immensely strong leader of the first race of gods—the Titans. His opposing counterpart was Zeus, who commanded the next generation of divine beings—the Olympians. Towering mountains crumbled and the seas boiled and bubbled as these dynamic and determined deities raged against one another for control of the universe.

Every ancient Greek boy and girl knew this exciting tale of the very first war, which, it was then widely believed, had taken place shortly after the earth's creation. Indeed, the residents of classical Greece repeatedly heard this and other creation stories almost from the moment they could talk. The term *classical Greece* was coined by modern historians to designate the Greeks of the era shortly before, during, and shortly after the fifth century BCE. It was they who produced an enormous burst of memorable culture that included the world's first democracies, theaters, and plays; the splendiferous Parthenon temple; and the immortal philosophical ideas of Plato, Socrates, and Aristotle.

Those now-famous few generations of Greeks inherited a large, splendid corpus, or collection, of myths from earlier residents of the region. So colorful and influential were these myths that, long after the ancient world faded from view, they continued to pass from one generation to another. And today they remain no less vivid and entertaining than they were millennia ago, the subjects of countless novels, comic books, movies, and TV shows.

Shortly after earth's creation, Zeus (armed with his signature thunderbolt) attacks the Titans in the furious battle for the universe.

From Darkness to Light

Among those unforgettable tales was the one about the clash of gods in the first war, along with other creation stories. The creation myths described how the gods fashioned the human race. Even before the Titans and Olympian gods themselves emerged, however, the universe—or cosmos, as the Greeks called it—sprang into being. Thus, the Greek conception of the creation was decidedly different from the ones portrayed by the Christians, Jews, Muslims, and Hindus.

Indeed, the late, great modern myth teller Edith Hamilton pointed out, the Greeks "did not believe that the gods created the universe. It was the other way about. The universe created the gods."[5]

The earliest form the cosmos took, according to the sixth-century-BCE Greek epic poet Hesiod, was a dark, swirling, dis-

Hesiod and His Muses

A great deal of what is known today about the ancient Greek version of the creation comes from the writings of Hesiod. One of Greece's two early, highly revered epic poets—the other being Homer—he most likely flourished in the late 700s and early 600s BCE. Although Hesiod's precise dates remain unknown, certain things he said in his two main works do indicate that he was a well-to-do farmer in Boeotia, the region of central Greece controlled by Thebes. One of those works, titled *Works and Days*, deals principally with agriculture. The other—the *Theogony*, or "Ancestry of the Gods"—goes into detail about the early Greek creation myths, including how the cosmos and the earth formed from Chaos and the rise of both the Titans and Olympian gods. In the work's introduction, Hesiod explains that he was inspired by the Muses, nine celestial daughters of the chief Olympian deity, Zeus. "Hail, daughters of Zeus!" the poet states. He implores them to tell him "how the gods and earth arose at first, and rivers and the boundless swollen sea and shining stars, and the broad heaven above, and how the gods divided up their wealth and how they shared their honors."

Hesiod, *Theogony*, in *Hesiod and Theognis*, trans. Dorothea Wender, New York: Penguin, 1982, p. 26.

organized collection of unknown substances. The Greeks called it Chaos. According to the late classical scholar W.H.D. Rouse, within that muddled mixture floated "the seeds or beginnings of all things [all] mixed up together in a shapeless mass, all moving about in all directions."[6]

For a long time—no one knows or will ever know just how long—the random reaches of Chaos remained blacker than the blackest night humans have ever witnessed. There was, in the words of the first-century-BCE Roman poet Ovid, only "the rounded body of all things in one," seemingly "the living elements at war with lifelessness."[7]

Then, within those circulating lifeless elements, something living suddenly stirred. Two conscious beings—formless and crude to be sure, yet alive nonetheless—became aware of their primitive surroundings, including each other. Later called Night and Erebus, they immediately formed a union in an effort to reproduce, a driving urge later shared by all living things. This attempt was successful, for after an unknown span of time had elapsed, Erebus felt an egg growing within her shapeless body.

Eros

The godlike being who emerged from Chaos and brought light to the cosmos; he was later seen as the god of love

Finally, the egg freed itself from its dark, barely conscious mother. For a while that kernel of potential new life remained as black and murky as the rest of Chaos. But eventually, and without warning, the egg suddenly burst open, releasing a new being, whom some Greeks later called God, others Nature, and still others Eros, meaning "Love." Whatever he was called, he emitted a flood of pure light that illuminated the spinning universal elements for the first time. God, in Ovid's words, "calmed those elements," giving them shape and meaning.

Land fell away from sky and sea from land, and air drew away from cloud and rain. As God unlocked all elemental things, fire climbed celestial vaults, air followed it to float in [the] heavens [and] earth, which carried all heavier things with it, dropped under air; and water fell farthest, embracing shores and islands. . . . At God's touch lakes, springs, dancing waterfalls streamed downhill into valleys, waters glancing through rocks, grass, and wild-flowered meadows.[8]

A Brilliant Organizer?

Thus did Eros bring forth light and create order from what had seemed hopeless disorder. There was now the earth's surface, with its chains of mountains, fertile plains and valleys, lakes and seas and rivers; and above loomed the sky, with clouds of different textures and hues, and above them the sun, moon, and stars. Also, below the earth's surface lay the dimly lit underworld, and beneath that the dark realm of Tartarus, where the gods would eventually imprison their enemies. In addition, the surface world became home to countless trees and other plants, along with thousands of animal species.

It must be stressed that the classical Greeks did not think Eros himself created the earth, sky, heavenly bodies, plants, and animals all out of nothing, as if by magic. Rather, they saw him more as a sort of brilliant organizer. He had emerged from a seed the cosmos itself had spawned. Similarly, the belief was that the seeds of mountains, lakes, plants, and animals had already existed within Chaos and that Eros somehow released and imparted order to them.

The Greeks also viewed the separation of the various primeval elements into tidy niches and categories as logical and to be expected. That is why Greek thinkers like Anaxagoras, Democritus, Plato, and Aristotle believed that nature seemed so complex and well thought out, even though, in their view, no thinking being had magically created it all. They and other Greek philosopher-scientists introduced the world's first scientific concepts. It appeared logical to them, based on their culture's creation myths, that natural laws had somehow been built into nature's structure, making it possible

Two High-Ranking Titans: Oceanus and Tethys

After Cronos and Rhea, perhaps the most important member of the earliest race of gods—the Titans—was Oceanus. The classical Greeks held that Oceanus controlled the large freshwater river—called the Ocean after him—that supposedly flowed around the outer boundaries of the earth's land portions. The Greeks also believed that this powerful deity strongly influenced the passage of time over the countless centuries following the creation. Still another role he played was to keep the sun, moon, and stars in their respective places in the sky so they would not fall down onto the earth's surface. One of the several Greek creation myths tells how Oceanus took control of all the waters in the world, including the many lakes, rivers, streams, human-made wells, and even the moisture within the clouds. His wife—another high-ranking Titan named Tethys—helped him with this large array of godly duties. Among other things, she frequently guided major portions of the world's waters through the vast caves that various myths said existed deep beneath the earth's surface.

for the cosmos to operate efficiently. In this way, the Greek creation myths indirectly influenced the rise of science in Western civilization.

Mother Earth and Father Heaven

The Greek notion of creation by spontaneous natural events, rather than by the purposeful intervention of a divine being, can also be seen in the next stage of the creation. As Hesiod told it, not long after Eros emerged and brought order to the youthful cosmos, two more powerful deities sprang into existence—or put another way, became conscious and self-aware. One was Gaia, a vast living spirit dwelling within the earth itself. The Greeks believed she was so perceptive that she was aware of almost everything that occurred on or near the earth's surface.

The other enormous spirit who achieved consciousness along with Gaia was Uranus, the personification of the sky that hung high above the earth. Sometimes called Father Heaven by the classical Greeks, he possessed three separate origin tales in the

Greek corpus of myths. In the first, he materialized and awakened of his own accord. The second account claimed he was the offspring of the primeval dark spirit Night. And the third and most popular version of his birth made him Gaia's own creation.

According to Hesiod, Gaia "the beautiful rose up, broad-bosomed, she that is the steadfast base of all things. And [she] first bore the starry Heaven, equal to herself, to cover her on all sides, and to be a home forever for the blessed gods."[9]

The early myths about Gaia and Uranus strongly influenced classical Greek religious and social customs, in part because these powerful nature spirits were the culture's original parental models. Typically, each new generation of Greeks seriously respected their parents. Moreover, it was common for a son or daughter to make a promise and swear to keep it on the life of his or her father or mother.

A Brood of Monsters

As the creation continued, like later mothers and fathers, Gaia and Uranus proceeded to mate and produce children. Initially, these offspring were what the classical Greeks saw, and people today see, as a brood of monsters. Some sported multiple heads or arms or were strange and misshapen in other ways. Others looked somewhat like humans in that they had one head, two arms, and two legs. However, these beings, called Cyclopes, were exceedingly ugly, and each had a single eye in the middle of its forehead.

Meanwhile, besides coupling with Uranus, the endlessly fertile and fruitful Gaia mated with Tartarus, the dark and scary lower portion of the underworld. From that weird union came still another monstrous creature—Echidna, described by Greek writers as having a woman's head and a snake's body. Another loathsome child spawned by Gaia and Tartarus was Typhon. The ancient

Greek myth teller known today as Pseudo-Apollodorus described the bizarre Typhon as the biggest and by far the

> strongest of all [Gaia's] children. Down to the thighs he was human in form, so large that he extended beyond all the mountains while his head often touched even the stars. One hand reached to the west, the other to the east, and attached to these were one hundred heads of serpents. Also from the thighs down he had great coils of vipers, which extended to the top of his head and hissed mightily. All of his body was winged, and the hair that flowed in the wind from his head and cheeks was matted and dirty. In his eyes flashed fire. Such were the appearance and the size of Typhon as he hurled red-hot rocks at the sky itself, and set out for it with mixed hisses and shouts, as a great storm of fire boiled forth from his mouth.[10]

In turn, Typhon coupled with its repulsive sibling, Echidna, bringing forth Cerberus, a huge doglike beast that most ancient

The muscular hero Heracles (whom the Romans later called Hercules) drags the doglike beast Cerberus up from its post at the underworld's outer border.

writers said had three heads. (Hesiod claimed it had fifty heads.) However many heads Cerberus may have had, his job eventually became standing guard at the underworld's borders and making sure that no shades, or human souls, dwelling there managed to escape. That "dreaded hound,"[11] in Hesiod's words, had not a shred of pity. If a soul did try to flee that dreary subterranean realm, Cerberus tracked it down and devoured it.

Completing the Majestic Cycle

In the next stage of the creation, Gaia and Uranus finally produced their most important, and physically most normal and attractive, offspring. Known as the Titans, they made up the first entire race of gods later recognized by the classical Greeks. Each of these deities had a single head, two arms, two legs, and two eyes. But though they possessed human form, the Titans were far from human in a number of ways. First, these early gods were immense, usually standing some 30 feet (9 m) tall, roughly five times the height of an average person. The Titans were also much more muscular and powerful than humans.

In addition, the Titans were blessed with special divine powers that no human would ever have. Most of those abilities were connected to the daily and yearly workings of the cosmos, the earth, and nature. Some Titans, for example, were tasked with maintaining the physical integrity of the earth, sky, stars, planets, and so forth. The god Iapetos, for instance, supposedly acted as a pillar holding up the sky in a spot far to the east of Greece. At the same time, Hyperion stood as a vital pillar in the west; Coeus in the north; and Crius in the south.

The leader of the Titans was Cronos, who, though not very bright, ensured the orderly passage of time. With his female mate, Rhea, Cronos begat a series of magnificent humanoid children, among them Poseidon, Hades, Hera, and Hestia. The strongest and smartest of that new generation, Zeus, saved his siblings from their father, who, fearing them, had swallowed them when they were infants. Zeus and his brothers and sisters then broke away from the Titans and became the second and most powerful divine race—the Olympians. The latter soundly defeated Cronos and his followers in the great war for control of the cosmos and imprisoned the surviving Titans in dismal Tartarus.

Not long afterward, Zeus assigned Prometheus, a Titan who had fought for the Olympians, a special project. It was to fashion

In this 1845 illustration, the Titan Prometheus fashions the first humans from mud, and Athena, goddess of wisdom and war, breathes life into the new creatures.

Prometheus

One of the Titans; he fashioned the human race from river mud

a race of mortal beings who would provide the gods with regular worship in the form of prayer, sacrifice, and annual religious festivals. Prometheus eagerly accepted the challenge and molded the first humans from lumps of river mud. When he was finished, the majestic cycle of creation—starting with a spinning mass of disordered elements and ending with the emergence of the human race—was finally complete.

CHAPTER TWO

The Creation According to the Babylonians

The Babylonians occupied the region often called Mesopotamia—what is now Iraq—during the second and first millennia BCE. Centered in one of the largest, most splendid cities of the ancient world—Babylon, on the Euphrates River—they had a diverse and rich collection of myths featuring numerous gods, monsters, and human heroes and villains. Some of those myths exerted a powerful influence on the early Hebrews and through them the Christian faith and culture that later emerged in the Roman Empire. A well-known example is the story of the great flood—initially a Mesopotamian tale, which eventually made its way into the Judeo-Christian Bible.

Most of the Babylonian gods and myths were not original to the Babylonians, who were themselves latecomers to Mesopotamia. Along with the Assyrians, who occupied Mesopotamia's northern plains, they constituted a direct offshoot of the first advanced people to inhabit the area—the Sumerians, who centuries before had erected the world's first cities there. In the words of the late, great scholar of ancient Mesopotamia Samuel N. Kramer, Sumerian culture "provided spiritual and ethical guidance for the affairs of men [and] bequeathed a heritage of colorful mythology that strongly influenced later religions. The Babylonians and Assyrians, who in their turn succeeded the Sumerians, took over most of the Sumerian gods and religious practices."[12]

Thus, even though the Sumerian city-states faded from power in the late 2000s BCE, Sumerian culture, including its gods and myths, remained deeply entrenched in the region. As a result, historian Jennifer Westwood points out, when people speak of Babylonian gods and myths, it would be more accurate to "call them something like Sumero-Babylonian. This is so clumsy, however, that most people simply speak of Babylonian myths," always keeping "in mind that many of these are of Sumerian origin."[13]

The New Year's Festival and *Enuma Elish*

A good example of this Sumerian-Babylonian connection is the leading Babylonian god, Marduk, known for organizing the universe and creating the human race, among other deeds. When Babylonian civilization reached its height of power and influence in the first millennium BCE, Marduk possessed numerous duties and abilities that centuries before had belonged to the Sumerian god Enlil. (The Babylonians still worshipped Enlil, but by that time he had been demoted to a weather god of far less stature; they called him Ellil.)

Marduk

The supreme Babylonian god, who created both the world and the human race

The Sumerians had celebrated a yearly religious festival in honor of Enlil, and the Babylonians caried on that tradition by holding an annual festival for Marduk on New Year's Day. The major highlight of that celebration was a reenactment by worshippers of the main events in Marduk's creation myth. The Babylonian king and his government sanctioned and funded that staged drama. As a result, the citizenry viewed it as the official and accurate version of how the world and humans came to be.

This is a modern artist's rendition of the Babylonian New Year's Day celebration. The highlight of the festival was a reenactment of the creation of the world by the great god Marduk.

For its details, the New Year's reenactment was closely and carefully based on a written creation epic—the *Enuma Elish*—which first appeared sometime between 1900 and 1600 BCE. Modern archaeologists discovered seven baked clay tablets bearing the work in some ruined Babylonian structures in 1849. The text was finally translated by the brilliant scholar George Smith in 1876, and people around the world were immediately struck by how closely parts of it resemble the creation story in the Bible's book of Genesis. The two works differ in some ways, to be sure. Yet the similarities are ample enough to show that the Babylonian document was indeed a key piece of source material for Genesis.

Marduk's Watery World

In a passage in the Babylonian creation epic, the *Enuma Elish*, excerpted here from W.G. Lambert's translation, after slaying his opponent, the goddess Tiamat, the young and mighty deity Marduk uses her bodily moisture to make the oceans, lakes, rivers, and other water sources of his new world, the earth.

> The foam which Tia-mat [had frothed from her mouth during the battle] Marduk fashioned [into something useful]. He gathered it together and made it into clouds. The raging of the winds, violent rainstorms, the billowing of mist—the accumulation of her spittle—[all of that] he appointed for himself and took them in his hand. [He] put her head in position and poured out [the moisture it contained]. He opened the abyss and it was sated with water. From her two eyes he let the Euphrates and Tigris [rivers] flow; he blocked her nostrils. . . . [Then] he heaped up the distant [mountains] on her breasts [to help keep the waters in place], and he bored wells to channel the springs.

W.G. Lambert, trans., *Enuma Elish*, World History Encyclopedia, 2018. www.worldhistory.org.

Apsu's Nefarious Plan

The title *Enuma Elish* came from the epic's opening words, which translate into English roughly as "When the heavens above." The first three of the work's approximately one thousand lines read: "When the heavens above did not exist, and earth beneath had not come into being, there was Apsu."[14] The Babylonian god of fresh water, Apsu supposedly existed long ago, at the dawn of time, before the universe and humans had been created. He was initially accompanied by some fellow divine beings who, like him, floated around in an enormous void filled with salt water. Among them were Tiamat, a guardian of that boundless sea; Lahmu, who would later have charge of the stars shining in the heavens at night; Anshar, the earliest god of the whole sky; and Anshar's mate, Kishar, a mother goddess who personified the earth itself, much as Gaia did in Greek mythology. Also present was Anu, Anshar and

Kishar's son, who over time took over most of his father's duties relating to the sky.

Although all of these deities played some role in setting the stage for the creation of the world and people, Apsu's actions first set that fateful process in motion.

After begetting Anu, the fertile Anshar and Kishar continued having divine offspring, and Anu himself had a son named Ea. After a few centuries, many dozens of heavenly beings eagerly interacted with one another, and the noise level of their chatter seriously annoyed both Apsu and Tiamat. At first, Tiamat was not inclined to resort to violence to remedy the situation, but after a while Apsu *was* so inclined. Finally feeling he could take no more of what he viewed as an infernal racket, he told Tiamat (in the *Enuma Elish*), "Their behavior has become displeasing to me, and I cannot rest in the day-time or sleep at night. I will destroy and break up their way of life, [in order] that silence may reign and we may sleep."[15]

After some initial reluctance, Tiamat expressed her support for the nefarious plan. Before Apsu could launch his attack, however, Ea found out about it and strongly objected. That upset Tiamat, who decided to punish Ea for interfering. To this end, she fashioned a throng of vile, monstrous creatures, including giant serpents with rows of sharp teeth. "They were merciless," the *Enuma Elish* states.

With poison instead of blood she filled their bodies. She clothed the fearful monsters with dread . . . she made them godlike. She said, "Let their onlooker feebly perish. May they constantly leap forward and never retire." She created the Hydra, the Dragon, the Hairy Hero, the Great Demon, the Savage Dog, and the Scorpion-man, fierce demons, the Fish-man, and the Bull-man, carriers of merciless weapons, fearless in the face of battle.[16]

A Stunning Victory and the Creation

The commander of this dreadful brigade was a repulsive character named Kingu. He and his followers, though not divine, were
nonetheless extremely strong and filled with hate, so Ea worried
that they might overpower him. Seeing the folly of facing the
monsters alone, he called on a powerful ally—his young son,
Marduk. Even though the latter was only a few months old at
the time, he was already a formidable figure and far stronger
than his father. All the other gods marveled at his courage and

*Marduk leads his forces against the rebellious Tiamat
and her ally, the evil creature Kingu. According to this
myth, Marduk chased down and slew Tiamat.*

skills. According to the *Enuma Elish*, Marduk's "figure was well developed, the glance of his eyes was dazzling, his growth was manly, [and] . . . his divinity was remarkable. [In addition] he became very lofty, excelling them [the other gods] in his attributes. [Overall, he was] incomprehensibly wonderful, incapable of being grasped with the mind, [and] hard even to look on."[17]

Some of the gods joined Ea and Marduk in the struggle that ensued. Despite his tender age, they gave Marduk complete charge of the group, and after he had clad himself in impenetrable armor, he confronted Tiamat and Kingu. Those wicked troublemakers quaked and shivered in fear when they beheld mighty Marduk, and hence the battle did not last long. Showing no mercy, Marduk chased down his fleeing enemies and slew all of them but Tiamat, who almost escaped. Finally, however, Marduk caught up to her and, according to a passage in the *Enuma Elish*, "with his merciless club [he] smashed her skull [and] severed her arteries."[18]

In the wake of his stunning victory over the forces of evil, Marduk decided to celebrate. What better way was there to do that, he reasoned, than to demonstrate his impressive powers in a surge of creative acts. Wasting no time, first he used his razor-sharp sword on Tiamat's enormous, lifeless body. "He split her in two like a dried fish," the Babylonian creation epic states. "One half of her he set up and stretched out as the heavens." The other half became the earth's surface. Then magnificent Marduk caused the moon to have phases, began the relentless progression of the seasons, and "set up constellations, the patterns of the stars. He appointed the year, marked off [sub]divisions [of it], and set up three stars each for the twelve months [and] organized the year."[19]

Even after watching their leader expend so much remarkable creative energy, the other gods were astonished to see that he was not yet finished. Now he skillfully fashioned humans by combining some clean clay from a riverbank with dead Kingu's blood. "I will bring together blood to form bone," Marduk announced (according to the *Enuma Elish*). "I will bring into being [a kind of being] whose name shall be 'man.' I will create man."[20]

Rise of the Esagila and Babylon

Astounded at what they had just witnessed, the other gods realized that they could never hope to match Marduk's strength, resourcefulness, and inventiveness. So they bowed before him and for more than an hour sang his praises. "No god can alter the utterance of his mouth," they said. "When he looks in fury, he does not relent; when his anger is ablaze, no god can face him; his mind is deep, his spirit is all-embracing."[21]

With the aid of some of the recently created humans, the gods also built a splendid, towering temple called the Esagila, whose name means "the shrine whose top is lofty." Around it, the great city of Babylon began to rise from the flatlands near the banks of the Euphrates. That sacred central structure, the gods told those earliest Babylonians, would henceforth be the focal point of human worship of Marduk and the other divinities.

With the temple and Babylon established, the cycle of creation Marduk had set in motion at last came to a close, and the memory of what had occurred remained intact as the official creation myth. The Babylonians, like the Sumerians before them, recognized what they viewed as several crucial and vital truths in that story. First, humanity had emerged through the kindly efforts of a generous god who had decisively overcome the forces of evil. That fact alone made people, whom Marduk had compassionately created, essentially morally good, like himself.

Second, in repayment for their creation by Marduk and his continued support of them, humans were expected to worship him and his fellow deities. The priests who ran the temple argued that this was both natural and fair. Indeed, they said, the very fact that people had been fashioned from a base, almost worthless material like clay indicated that they were by their nature base and therefore must be servile to the heavenly beings. This, Samuel N. Kramer wrote, explains why the Babylonians believed

> they were created to be slaves and servants of the gods
> [and] accepted the divine decisions, even the inexplicable

and seemingly unjustified ones. . . . [People were] taught [from birth] not to argue and complain in the face of inscrutable [unexplained] misfortune. [Moreover] because of people's subservient position in relation to the gods, it was vitally important that they honor the gods on certain important occasions.[22]

The splendid Esagila temple formed the centerpiece of ancient Babylon. Other structures were likely built nearby, although the existence of at least one—the Hanging Gardens of Babylon (pictured)—has never been confirmed.

The most significant of those occasions was the advent of the new year, when priests read aloud and reenacted the creation myth. Such celebrations took place not only at the Esagila in Babylon but also at other religious shrines across Mesopotamia. In Babylon itself, after the *Enuma Elish* portion of the festivities was completed, the Babylonian king rode in a jewel-covered chariot at the head of a magnificent procession. It included other high government officials and the leading priests. They solemnly marched through the local streets, exited the city through the Ishtar Gate, and made their way to a special shrine on the riverbank. After three days of prayers and sacrifices to the gods, the participants returned to the Esagila.

Living by Heaven-Sent Rules

Based on their creation myths, the residents of ancient Babylon held that the deities they worshipped had not only fashioned the human race but also introduced rules to govern both nature and human society. The Babylonians called these rules *parsu*. (Their predecessors in Mesopotamia, the Sumerians, called those regulations *me*, pronounced MAY.) The *parsu* described the manner in which religious rituals should be conducted. They also defined the proper approach to government policies, military campaigns, arts and crafts, and even sexual relations. Most Babylonians and other inhabitants of Mesopotamia were grateful for these rules because they constituted a sort of reassurance that order and decency existed in what was otherwise a troubled and at times dangerous world. In the words of the late historian Samuel N. Kramer, people

> needed to believe that the universe and all its parts, once created, would continue to operate in an orderly and effective manner, not subject to disintegration and deterioration. The [heaven-sent statutes] governed everyone and everything in the universe, and mortal men could take comfort in the knowledge that the blue sky, the teeming earth . . . [and] the wild sea, were all acting in accordance with the rules of the gods.

Samuel N. Kramer, *Cradle of Civilization*. New York: Time-Life, 1978, p. 102.

Humanity Reassured by Myths

The care and reverence the Babylonians put into that yearly celebration of the creation myth shows how important it, and sacred myths in general, were to that society. As H.W.F. Saggs put it, the epic of creation gave people

> reassurance of the unchanging continuance of the world as the Babylonians knew it. The old primordial forces were still there to maintain the universe, but with their destructive elements bound and their kindly aspect harnessed for humanity's benefit. . . . The course of the unchanging month and year was fixed forever by the moon and stars, [Humans'] own place was assured, for were they not created for the service of the gods? And Babylon itself and its [religious] cults and institutions stood, splendid and eternal, the creations of the gods themselves.[23]

CHAPTER THREE

The Creation According to the Aztecs

Today, when most people in Western society hear the word *myths*, they envision the gods and legends of the ancient Greeks, Romans, Norse, Celts, and other inhabitants of the early European sphere. However, non-European peoples around the globe had equally extensive and rich mythologies of their own. In Mesoamerica (ancient Mexico and Central America), for example, complex, colorful myths, including creation stories, abounded.

Particularly memorable are the creation myths of the last major native Mesoamerican people to thrive before the European conquest of the area in the 1500s—the Aztecs. They called themselves the Mexica. (The term *Aztec* was coined in 1810 by a noted German naturalist.) During the 1300s to 1500s, they carved out a large-scale empire that covered much of Mexico and Central America and included numerous subservient native peoples.

A factor that made the Aztec creation myths so distinctive and compelling was their firm belief that the military and political successes that had led to their supremacy in the region were no accident. Rather, those events were long before ordained by the gods, who supposedly viewed the Mexica/Aztecs as "chosen" among all other peoples. In other words, because they were blessed by the gods, it was inevitable that the Aztecs would rule what they saw as the known world.

Partly for this reason, the Aztecs were even more preoccupied with stories about creation and the beginnings of things than most of the world's other cultures. How had the gods, especially the Aztec national patron deity, Huitzilopochtli, come to be, they wondered? How did the life-giving sun first appear in the sky? These were only a couple of the questions they found answers for in ancient myths.

The Lord and Lady of Duality

This obsession with tales of beginnings partially explains why the Aztecs developed multiple creation stories. California State University scholar Manuel Aguilar-Moreno explains that they rec-

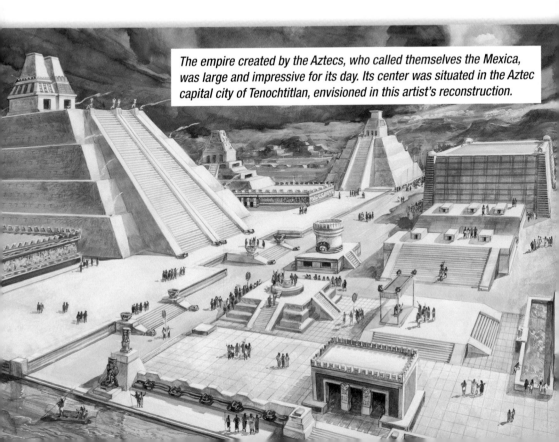

The empire created by the Aztecs, who called themselves the Mexica, was large and impressive for its day. Its center was situated in the Aztec capital city of Tenochtitlan, envisioned in this artist's reconstruction.

ognized the existence of several past ages and worlds, each of which perished and led to the rise of a new society.

The previous worlds, known as "Suns," were each created out of destruction. Each Sun's demise was due to a named catastrophe prompted by a fight between [two] conflicting deities, Quetzalcoatl, representing life, fertility, and light, and Black Tezcatlipoca, representing darkness and war. Each cataclysm [brought] an end to the world and death to all of its inhabitants. Out of death and destruction, however, a new and better world was born, in which humanity lived in a more perfect stage than that of the previous Suns.[24]

In the Aztecs' worldview, however, none of the four Suns marked the *very* beginning of the universe. The societies that arose during the long period of the Suns were essentially later echoes, or newer versions, of an original creation that took place at the beginning of time. The principal orchestrator of that initial act of creation was a powerful being named Ometeotl. This being possessed an unusual characteristic. Ometeotl was both male and female at the same time. For that reason, people routinely called Ometeotl the Lord and Lady of Duality. The theme of dual, conflicting attributes in a single deity is plainly addressed in an ancient Aztec song, the lyrics of which state in part, "He/She is the mirror of day and night. He/She is the star which illumines all things and he/she is the Lady of the shining skirt of stars. He/She is our mother, our father. Above all, he/she is Ometeotl, who dwells in the place of duality, Omeyocan [the highest level of Heaven]. . . . He/She is mother and father of the gods, the old god."[25]

A particularly outstanding and odd facet of this deity's duality was that, because of being both male and female, Ometeotl fea-

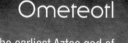

Ometeotl

The earliest Aztec god of creation, who possessed both male and female characteristics

tured the reproductive equipment of both men and women. That made it possible for Ometeotl to mate with himself/herself. Indeed, in the creation myth in which he/she is the main character, Ometeotl did just that, and in so doing initiated the creation of the universe. The first things made in this way were four more divine beings, all male, bearing the names Tezcatlipoca, Xipe Totec, Quetzalcoatl, and Huitzilopochtli.

The War God's Conflicting Birth Stories

People learning about Aztec mythology for the first time are often confused about how Ometeotl could have given birth to the war god Huitzilopochtli. This is because another, equally famous myth

The Four Suns of Creation

The first four Suns, or early ages, in the Aztec creation myths featured various gods ruling separate civilizations, each of which had humanlike beings and ended in complete catastrophe. During the first age, or Jaguar Sun, Tezcatlipoca administered the world, in which the inhabitants were giants who sustained themselves by eating acorns. That era ended when Quetzalcoatl drove Tezcatlipoca away and some huge jaguars devoured the giants. Quetzalcoatl then took charge of the second age, the Wind Sun. His worshippers were normal-sized people who survived on nuts. A few centuries went by before Tezcatlipoca got revenge by transforming the nut eaters into monkeys. To drive him away, Quetzalcoatl unleashed destructive storms, but these storms also destroyed the world. The third age, or Rain Sun, was ruled by the rain god, Tlaloc, whose worshippers subsisted on water lilies. This time the world ended when the still furious Tezcatlipoca stole Tlaloc's first wife, and Tlaloc retaliated by scorching the earth's surface with fire. Finally, the fourth age—the Water Sun—arose with Tlaloc's second spouse, Chalchiuhtlicue, in charge. Once more, Tezcatlipoca was the villain of the story. He pushed Chalchiuhtlicue out of the sky, which then exploded, releasing so much water that the earth was completely flooded.

claimed Huitzilopochtli came into existence in a different manner. Namely, that deity was supposedly the offspring of Coatlícue, goddess of the earth itself.

The reason for this apparent contradiction is an example of how the Aztecs subtly manipulated their creation myths to suit various cultural and political needs and circumstances. First, prior to the Aztecs' arrival in central Mexico, a majority of the peoples who dwelled there revered the creation tale involving Ometeotl. The Aztecs were at that point unfamiliar with it but decided to make it part of their lore as a way of fitting in among the locals.

This colorful image, drawn by ancient Aztec artists for a codex, or book, depicts the patron deity of that people—Huitzilopochtli. The Aztecs envisioned him as the god of the sun as well as the overseer of battles and war.

Also, before the Aztecs entered the region from somewhere to the north, Huitzilopochtli was *not* among Ometeotl's four sons in the story. Instead, Huitzilopochtli was the personal patron deity of the Aztecs themselves. It troubled them that the region's most widely accepted creation myth did not mention their patron's divinity, so they substituted him for one of the original four gods in the story. That elevated their national god to the same level of importance as Tezcatlipoca, Quetzalcoatl, and Xipe Totec.

Clearly, an important result of these events was the fact that two versions of Huitzilopochtli's birth now existed. One featured his mother, the earth goddess Coatlícue, and the other claimed he was the fourth son of the creator deity Ometeotl. Wisely, the Aztecs accepted and celebrated both of those birth legends. Although most people today would view that as illogical, Aztec priests argued that it had a certain logic and credibility. They pointed out an aspect of their belief system that does not exist in most world religions. It was that although the gods were immortal in the long run, they could and did sometimes die, soon after which they were reborn. An inevitable consequence of that idea was that a single god might be born in a different way in each lifetime. That neatly explained how Huitzilopochtli had two seemingly conflicting birth stories.

Ometeotl's Four Divine Assistants

In the myth in which Huitzilopochtli was Ometeotl's offspring, each of the latter's four sons was associated with a different color. Huitzilopochtli's color was blue, Tezcatlipoca's was black, Quetzalcoatl's was white, and Xipe Totec's was red. As might be expected, Aztec artists regularly depicted these beings wearing outfits that featured their respective mythical colors.

The paintings showing those colorful divinities frequently depicted them carrying out acts of creation often assigned to them by their father/mother, Ometeotl. Thus, the four acted as his/her assistants in those monumental projects. One of the biggest was the creation of a vast sea. To populate it, at least temporarily, the

Nata, Nena, and Noah

Among the Aztec creation myths was one that resembled portions of the Bible's famous tale of the great flood, Noah, and the ark. The Aztec version takes place near the end of the fourth age, the Water Sun. The god Tezcatlipoca appears to a human couple and warns them that an enormous flood will soon threaten the world. The god suggests that the husband and his wife, Nata and Nena, construct a big boat from a cypress tree. That would hopefully allow them to survive the deluge. Nata and Nena thank the deity and build the vessel, after which the flood arrives. Safe on the ship, the couple watches the land portions of the earth disappear beneath the waves. When the catastrophe finally ends, the boat floats aimlessly for a few days, and Nata and Nena grow quite hungry. So they catch some fish and eagerly consume them. At that moment, Tezcatlipoca reappears and scolds them for eating the fish. He explains that during the flood some gods had transformed the other people in that society into fish, so the couple had actually eaten some fellow humans. To punish them, Tezcatlipoca turns them into dogs.

four divine brothers fashioned a massive, impressive, but unfortunate sea creature known as Cipactli. The reason it was unfortunate is that mere days after creating it, the four gods assaulted it and tore it apart into several large fragments. One piece became the sky, which had multiple layers, one bearing clouds, another the stars, and so forth. Another of Cipactli's remains became the earth's broad, flat disk, covered by mountains, valleys, forests, and lakes and surrounded by individual oceans (which though large by human standards were small compared to the initial sea that held Cipactli).

In Nahuatl, the Aztecs' language, the enormous expanse of land making up the earth and its surrounding oceans was called Cemanahuac. A literal translation is "the land surrounded by water." The Aztecs assumed that Mexico, along with some little-known lands lying south of it, constituted the whole earth. This view was supported by the fact that they could readily observe seemingly boundless oceans in the west and east and because they had no idea that other continents existed.

Still another fragment of Cipactli's gigantic body that the four divine brothers recycled became Mictlan, the mysterious under-ground realm of the dead. The Aztecs believed that the creator gods also manufactured two new deities to rule and administer dreary Mictlan. One was a skeleton-like creature named Mictlan-tecuhtli; the other was his no less unsightly wife, Mictecacihuatl.

Having created those two gods, Ometeotl's four assistants proceeded to make several more. They included Xochiquetzal, goddess of corn, flowers, and sexual relations; Tlaloc, her hus-band and the god of rain; and Chalchiuhtlicue, the guardian spirit of rivers, lakes, wells, and other water sources. The four creators also set up a complex system of the passage of days, weeks, and months, along with a calendar to keep track of them all.

Ages in Chaos

These and the other new gods that came into being this way mar-veled at the great surge of creative energy expended by Ometeo-tl's four sons. However, that resourceful and admirable achieve-ment was eventually marred by a major disagreement among the four creators. On the one hand, they all agreed that it was neces-sary to fashion a shining sun to produce the energy required to provide warmth and help crops grow. On the other, they heatedly squabbled over which of them would become the sun god and divine ruler of the newly created universe.

What had begun as strictly a verbal quarrel soon deteriorated into physical violence. The four creators now fought openly for supremacy during the so-called Suns, each a centuries-long era in which a different god ruled. In the words of the late Mexican historian Miguel Leon-Portilla, each god loudly claimed to be the rightful sun god so that he could "direct the destiny of the world." During each Sun, its ruler created local mortal worshippers and strove for peace. But inevitably, "at the end of each age, war broke out [and] destruction followed,"[26] including the annihilation of the worshippers.

The Aztecs believed that they dwelled in the fifth age. Because the prior four eras had each devolved into chaos and ended in disaster, they reluctantly accepted the idea that their own age would also someday come to a violent end. Successive generations of Aztec priests predicted that at some point in the future, the mountains would crumble and horrible monsters would appear, track down, and consume the few humans who might still be alive.

Their Most Inspiring Creation Myth

Furthermore, a crucial series of events that supposedly occurred during the rise of the fifth Sun led to the creation of the version of humanity that still exists today. Those events also contributed to the development of perhaps the most important, or at least the most memorable, of the Aztec religious customs. The first of those fateful events took place right after a great flood had destroyed the world of the fourth age. A group of concerned gods met to fashion a new race of humans to populate that society.

To make sure that the new humans would have a warm, reliable sun, the gods concluded that some of those deities must sacrifice their own lives by jumping into a big fire. This would transform them into a blazing, enduring sun. A Spanish priest who lived among the Aztecs in the late 1500s wrote an account that described how the moon god, Tecuciztecatl, volunteered to be the first to die for humanity. "O Gods," he cried out, "I will be the one." At first, no one else dared. Finally, however, "a god named Nanauatzin [stepped forward and] the gods called to him and said, 'You shall be the one.' He eagerly accepted the decision, saying, 'It is well, O gods.'"[27]

Tecuciztecatl and Nanauatzin then leaped into the fire. Thanks to their brave sacrifice, the next morning a brilliant, warm

This illustration from an Aztec codex shows an example of human sacrifice, in which priests removed the victim's heart. The original image was painted on vellum, or animal skin.

sun appeared on the horizon, and the other gods rejoiced. But then they noticed another problem. The new sun stayed on the horizon and did not move across the sky. After more discussion, they agreed that to make the sun move properly, they must *all* jump into the flames. They did so, and although they were all reborn later, they had demonstrated incredible courage and suffered terrible agony.

The Aztecs were tremendously inspired by this myth. They decided that they must pay back the gods for that valiant gesture, and this became the basis for their custom of human sacrifice. As historian Michael E. Smith explains, "just as these gods sacrificed themselves for the sun, so too people had to provide blood and hearts to keep the sun going."[28] The Spaniards who conquered the Aztecs saw human sacrifices as barbaric, whereas the Aztecs viewed them as fair, necessary, and a logical outgrowth of their sacred creation myth. It is doubtful that in all the world there has existed a myth that more directly and dramatically affected the everyday lives of a past people.

CHAPTER FOUR

The Creation According to the Hindus

Hinduism, centered mainly in India and other parts of Asia, is the world's third-largest faith, after Christianity and Islam. The ancient Indians who initiated Hinduism passed on to later generations some of the most colorful creation myths in world history. The basic elements of those tales are very ancient. The stories slowly and steadily grew more detailed during the many centuries that preceded the emergence, circa 500 BCE (about 2,500 years ago), of the religion that modern Hindus still follow.

Indeed, that faith and the culture it was a part of, so-called classical Hinduism, developed out of two prior advanced Indian civilizations. The first, often called Harappan culture, reached its height between 3000 and 2600 BCE along the banks of the Indus River (in an area of what is now Pakistan). The Harappans erected a number of flourishing cities and dwelled in well-built brick houses aligned along streets laid out in modern-looking grids. For reasons that remain somewhat unclear, that culture declined, and after roughly 1900 BCE the Harappans abandoned their cities.

In time, the survivors, who lived in small villages, regrouped. In the process they created an altered version of the former culture. This second Indian civilization, which thrived from about 1500 to 500 BCE, became known as Vedic culture. The Vedic religion, which was likely partially based on Harappan beliefs, featured several gods and beliefs that later became bedrock principles of classical Hinduism. Vedic priests set down these ideas in a series of sacred writings—the Vedas—which remain important documents in Hinduism even today.

A modern illustration captures a scene from everyday life in India's first advanced civilization—today most often called Harappan culture. The Harappans erected a number of cities in the Indus Valley (now mainly Pakistan).

Time's Cycles and Subcycles

In the principal Hindu creation tale, the dawn triggered by Vishnu's awakening is not actually the first dawn that ever occurred. Instead, it is the latest of an infinite number of dawns, each marking the start of a new universe. In Hinduism, the cosmos and time itself are perpetual and unending and therefore have no clear-cut beginning or end. They are cyclic. And in each new cycle, the gods and human civilization are born, flourish for a while, and then decline and vanish, making way for the next cycle of creation. No one knows how long each cycle lasts. But most Hindu thinkers suspect that a single cycle can last billions of years. They usually divide that immense time period into several shorter, more manageable subcycles, the smallest being the *kalpa*. In the words of noted English mythologist Veronica Ions, a *kalpa* is "one mere day in the life of Brahma, but is equivalent to 4.32 billion years on earth. When Brahma wakes, the three worlds (heavens, middle, and lower regions) are created, and when he sleeps, they are reduced to chaos."

Veronica Ions, *Indian Mythology*. New York: Peter Bedrick, 1984, p. 24.

Avatars of the Sole God

A fairly large portion of Hindu mythology, including a few stories about the creation of the world, appear in the Vedas. Later, after Hinduism fully developed, more advanced and detailed versions of those older creation stories came about. These stories differ from Judeo-Christian and Islamic creation stories in a crucial way. The so-called Abrahamic faiths—Judaism, Christianity, and Islam—envision the beginning of all things as happening in a single, unambiguous event. In it, God suddenly created the earth and the heavens in six days. Implicit in that belief is the notion that before God did that, nothing except for God himself had ever existed.

In contrast, Hindu mythology features multiple creations, each preceded and followed by others, so that some sort of universe has *always* existed. In the Hindu vision of creation, therefore, the cosmos, along with time itself, is everlasting, with no distinct beginning or end. Each new world emerges, flourishes for a while, and eventually declines and disappears, opening the way for the birth of a new world, which also ultimately declines.

Thus, a fundamental difference between the Hindu concept of creation and the one envisioned in the Abrahamic faiths is the number of creation events—one versus an infinite number. However, there are some similarities between the two visions. The main, and most important, similarity lies in the concept of the creator—that is, God. Many Jews, Christians, and Muslims are surprised when they learn that the Hindu concept of God is much like their own. Contrary to popular belief, Hinduism is *not* polytheistic, or based on the idea of the existence of multiple, completely separate and distinct gods. Rather, Hindus believe that the thousands of deities recognized in Hindu myths, worship, and artworks are all incarnations (manifestations, disguises, or avatars) of a single, all-powerful god. They call this god Brahman, as well as the *ishvara*, or universal spirit. One modern Hindu priest and scholar describes Brahman as formless and "Pure Consciousness, [a] primal substance, pure love, and light flowing through all form, existing everywhere in time and space as infinite intelligence and power. . . . [Brahman] protects, nurtures and guides us. We beseech God's grace in our lives while also knowing that He/She is the essence of our soul, the life of our life."[29]

Brahman

The sole Hindu god, whose avatars created the universe

A Flower Floating in a Vast Ocean

For reasons that no human has ever fathomed, the Hindu sole god, Brahman, decided always to relate to humanity through his diverse incarnations. That fact is an essential component of the principal Hindu creation story, for in that tale God works in the guise of two of his three most powerful and famous avatars. They are Brahma (not to be confused with his larger self, the sole god

Brahman) and Vishnu. (Along with another god, Shiva, they make up Hinduism's holy trinity—the Trimurti.)

That principal creation myth begins with Brahma awakening from what feels to him like a long sleep. Glancing around, he sees that he is wrapped in the leaves of a very large lotus flower; moreover, that blossom is floating atop an immense, dark ocean that stretches away to the horizon in all directions. No land or sky or anything else is visible. Brahma climbs out of the flower and realizes that he neither falls downward nor rises upward, but rather continues to hover in the same place.

Not long afterward, Brahma catches sight of something on the water's surface floating toward him. When it gets close enough to see clearly, he realizes it is a very large snake. Maneuvering closer still, he sees something intertwined within the serpent's coils and a few seconds later recognizes that it is the god Vishnu. The latter is fast asleep, and Brahma decides that it will be best to let his fellow avatar continue napping until he is fully rested, however long that happens to be.

Vishnu

The so-called Preserver god, who helped his fellow god, Brahma, create the earth and the heavens

While watching the dozing deity, Brahma notices something else in the vast ocean—a strange humming sound. As time goes by, it grows louder and louder until it is nearly deafening, and Brahma is not surprised that it awakens Vishnu. As that handsome being opens his eyes, a flood of light washes over the sea. The bright disk of a sun hangs on the horizon, and it is clear to both gods that the first dawn of a new age has arrived.

The two gods feel compelled to begin a major round of creation. The first thing they do is split Brahma's lotus into three parts, one of which rapidly transforms into the earth's surface. The flower's second section rises up and becomes the sky, and the third one floats higher still and morphs into a heavenly sphere studded with stars. Those flowing orbs introduce fire into the new cosmos, and air fills the voids between the earth and sky and the sky and the heavenly vault.

A modern painting depicts the central images of the main Hindu creation story. They include the gods Brahma and Vishnu, reclining on a large lotus flower, which itself rests atop the coils of a giant serpent.

Gods, Animals, Plants, and More

Having fashioned the major components of the new universe, Brahma and Vishnu feel themselves seemingly bursting with creative energy. It is almost as if they cannot contain their enthusiasm to fill the new world with living things. They start by making avatars of themselves, along with other incarnations of the almighty *ishvara*, some of which have their own avatars. In this way a large number of gods and goddess appear, prominent among them the elephant-headed Ganesha, god of wisdom; Parvati, goddess of love; and Lakshmi, goddess of beauty and wealth.

Some of these divinities lend a hand with the ongoing creation, following Brahma's instructions, which makes the grandiose project move forward even faster. As a result, in the words of popular modern myth teller Donna Rosenberg, "the earth, which

Ganesha

The elephant-headed Hindu god of wisdom, who championed the arts and was thought to remove obstacles in life

45

was barren to begin with, rapidly fills with living things." These include "goats from [Brahma's] mouth, sheep from his chest, cows from his stomach, antelope, buffalo, camels, donkeys, elephants, and other animals from his arms and legs, horses from his feet, and plant life from the hair on his body."[30] Assorted insects, reptiles, birds, and sea creatures also arise.

Thus ends one of the main creation myths of Hinduism. It contains explanations for how large numbers of gods, natural elements, animals, and plants arose. The ancient Hindus saw these as very positive achievements. They also recognized that certain negative beings and elements exist in the world. To account for their beginnings, some other creation myths evolved, including one that claimed that those bad things resulted from some unfortunate errors Brahma made. Supposedly, at one point he became distracted momentarily, and that allowed an intelligent force called Ignorance to arise.

After its emergence, Ignorance continued to evolve and did some creating of its own. It birthed various evil forces and creatures, some of which still exist today. Hoping to keep those bad things in check, Brahma fashioned angel-like beings that thereafter opposed, though were unable to completely destroy, the evil elements.

In a second alternate version of the main creation tale, Ignorance was not a character. The world's darker forces, including sinful urges and demons, instead sprang from Brahma's thigh one day while he slept. After that, New Jersey Institute of Technology professor Mark Cartwright writes, the mortified Brahma "abandoned his own body which then became Night. After Brahma created [some more] good gods, he abandoned his body once again, which then became Day, hence demons gain the ascendancy at night and gods, the forces of goodness, rule the day."[31]

The Rise of Humanity

At the point when Brahma, to some degree aided by Vishnu, had finished making the earth, the sky, air, mountains, forests, animals, and plants, the task of creation was nearly done. But

46

The Chief Hindu Gods

The two gods who do most of the work in the best-known Hindu creation tale—Brahma and Vishnu—are also among the leading Hindu deities overall. In the Vedic age (ca. 1500–500 BCE), which directly preceded the emergence of full-blown Hindu culture, the principal god was Indra. A powerful nature deity who wielded thunderbolts as weapons, he closely resembled the Greek Zeus and Norse Thor. However, the Hindus elevated Brahma and Vishnu well above Indra, who was thereafter a weather god of minor importance. In the Hindu pantheon, Brahma, often called the Creator, and Vishnu, known as the Preserver, along with Shiva, the Destroyer, were the most revered avatars of the universal spirit. Hindus came to group these three gods together, forming a divine trinity. In the Hindu faith, that sacred group is called the Trimurti. Of its three members, Brahma was most associated with acts of creation. Although Vishnu aided in those endeavors, he is better known for maintaining the integrity of the existing order. Meanwhile, Shiva's main role was to dismantle or erase outdated or useless aspects of the universe.

Brahma felt there was something missing. Thinking about it for a few minutes, it came to him. He realized that it was essential to fashion a race of humans, both to enjoy all those natural wonders and to worship the many manifestations of the sole deity.

To that end, Brahma made the first person—a man he called Manu. Both Brahma and Vishnu viewed that creature as fascinating, so for a while they kept a close eye on his activities. As they watched, one day Manu strolled along the bank of the Indus River. Suddenly, he heard a noise that seemed out of place and stopped to listen more closely. It was a faint little voice, which cried out for aid. After searching the area, Manu found the source of the voice—a small fish flopping around on the riverbank. The creature was clearly relieved to see Manu and implored him to thereafter keep it as a pet, which would help keep it from being devoured by larger fish. Taking pity on what appeared to be a defenseless little being, Manu said he would care for the fish by placing it in a bucket of water.

It seemed only right to the fish that it should repay Manu for his kindness. So a few days later, the little creature told his human companion a secret that supposedly only animals knew. Namely, a gigantic flood was soon going to sweep across the earth's surface. To escape this catastrophe, the fish continued, Manu's only hope was to build a boat that would float atop the water's surface.

Believing what the fish told him, Manu proceeded to craft a wooden vessel big enough to accommodate himself, the fish's

In the story of the great flood, Manu is guided by a fish who eventually reveals that it is really an avatar, or disguise, of the preserver-god Vishnu.

bucket, and some basic supplies. The man was soon grateful to his little friend because the deluge did come and, just as predicted, covered the dry land from horizon to horizon. The little boat floated in the floodwater for more than a week, until the water subsided.

When Manu finally stepped out of the boat, something extraordinary occurred. The fish underwent a rapid transformation into a wondrous being who glowed with a bluish radiance. "I am Vishnu, the Preserver," the being told Manu (as described in the Hindu epic poem the *Bhagavad-Gita*). "I appeared to you in the shape of a fish to protect you from the deluge. You are destined to start new races to inhabit the world."[32]

To ensure that destiny, Brahma visited Manu. The god brought with him a young woman he had created to be Manu's wife. Her name, Brahma said, was Shatarupa. In the years that followed, she and Manu had several offspring, who themselves had more children; in turn, those people reproduced too, as they spread outward over the earth's surface. This process marked the rise of humanity.

Hymn to the True Creator

Finally, Brahma and the divine avatars who had aided him felt like they could rest for a while. The majestic process of creation that had begun in a vast, dimly lit sea was at last finished. The early humans created by Brahma, Vishnu, and other heavenly beings came to realize that those gods were merely projections, or echoes, of the sole, almighty god Brahman. The true creator, for his own reasons he had chosen not to reveal his true form. Hoping to reach out to him with thanks and praise, those first people in the new age composed a hymn (first recorded in one of the Vedas). It reads in part, "You are invisible, too enigmatic [mysterious] to be perceived, infinite, most ancient of all. You are hidden where nothing can be concealed. . . . Nothing can exist without your wish. Our [thankful] wishes we present to you. . . . You are the truest friend that all look for. [Please] heartily accept this poet's prayer."[33]

CHAPTER FIVE

The Creation According to the Chinese

Chinese mythology features several entertaining creation myths that are still told and retold today. They originated in a very ancient culture that modern historians call one of the four "cradles of civilization," all rich cultures that grew up along the banks of major rivers. (The other three cradles were in Egypt, along the Nile River; Mesopotamia, in today's Iraq, along the Tigris and Euphrates Rivers; and India, along the Indus River.) The Chinese cradle appeared in the mid-to-late 2000s BCE somewhere along the Yellow River, in northeastern China.

Initially most Chinese lived in small agricultural villages that took advantage of the fertile soil the river had laid down over time in its wide, rain-swept valley. The gods worshipped by the early inhabitants of this region remain largely shrouded in the midst of time. The ancient Chinese gods known today were the ones worshipped after the first organized kingdoms, each ruled by an emperor, arose around 1600 BCE. Historians divide the centuries of Chinese history that followed into time periods called dynasties. Each dynasty comprised the combined reigns of a line of rulers who were related by blood. (Thus, a dynasty is a family line of rulers.)

The first dynasty—the Shang (ca. 1600–1050 BCE)—is thought to have introduced social customs and religious rituals, gods, and myths that people perpetuated throughout the remainder of the region's history. At first, the myths were told and retold strictly orally; that is, by word of mouth. When the Chinese did begin writing down their myths about a millennium later (during 300 to 200 BCE), a number of detailed, colorful creation stories existed.

As in the case of most mythologies, some of the Chinese ones describe the beginnings of the universe and human race. One way that the Chinese creation myths differ from those of most other peoples is that the ancient Chinese viewed another aspect of creation as being equally important. That aspect is the origin of human culture, encompassing language, arts and crafts, religious ideas, and social and legal concepts. The Chinese have "abundant myths about culture heroes and their inventions," scholar Lihui Yang writes. "These inventions refer to the ordering of human life; acquisition of a livable environment; acquisition of a food supply for humans; creation of crafts, arts, and wisdom; establishment of customs and laws; and so on."[34]

The God from the Egg

Another way that Chinese creation myths differ from those of other peoples is that the Chinese seemed to have little or no interest in where the gods, including the creator deities, came from. More often it was assumed that such a god had somehow always existed. Or else no human could ever fathom how he, she, or it had originated.

A clear example of this assumption is the way the creator appears in the most-often repeated Chinese tale of the beginning of the universe. That creator, who was also the first of the numerous Chinese deities, was known as Pangu. The Chinese scholar Xu Zheng, who flourished in the 200s CE, was the first ancient writer to tell Pangu's story. It begins with a seemingly

Pangu

The very first Chinese god, he was said to have fashioned the earth and the heavens from remnants of a cosmic egg

A nineteenth-century engraving shows the ancient Chinese creator deity Pangu carving out the earth. A popular tale claims he did this after emerging from thousands of years of slumber within an egg.

unlimited expanse of darkness, within which unidentified, chaotic forces swirled around and around. Only a single well-defined object existed at that time—an extremely large egg. How it got there is anyone's guess; the crucial point is that it existed and occupied the center of all that was.

Even more important was what dwelled within that cosmic egg. Fast asleep inside was the divine spirit that came to be known as Pangu. He must have hugely enjoyed sleeping because he did so for some eighteen thousand years. Finally, however, according to the myth teller for the Chinese ballet company Shen Yun, Pangu "suddenly awoke. He opened his eyes, but saw only pitch-blackness. He strained his ears, but heard only unnerving silence. Pan Gu found his dreary surroundings highly disturbing. Flustered, he conjured a magical ax and landed upon the egg a mighty chop. The egg split into two with a thunderous crack."[35]

In all those thousands of years, Pangu must have been growing larger a little at a time, because when he broke free of that primal prison, he was nothing less than enormous. He was also extremely hairy. Ancient Chinese artists often depicted him wearing a bearskin, similar to the way the Greco-Roman hero Hercules wore the skin of a lion he had slain. Various painters also depicted Pangu as having the head of a dog or a human head with horns extending outward from its sides.

A Miraculous Transformation

Some of these visions of Pangu's physical appearance may be accurate, or perhaps none of them are. The truth is that no one can be sure what he looked like because by the time people came along, the first god was no longer on earth. Therefore, no human ever saw him in person.

Much more important than Pangu's appearance is what he did. Having broken free of the cosmic egg, he used his mighty ax to slice up its remains, and the lighter sections drifted upward and became the sky. In contrast, the heavier parts descended downward and formed the earth's solid surface. In this way, Pangu brought order to what had been disorder, a process that took him another eighteen thousand years. So dedicated was he to this task that he never rested or took a break to eat or sleep; hence, when he was finally finished, he was completely exhausted. Nevertheless, he was satisfied that he had done the job well. Thinking that it would be impossible to do anything more worthwhile than this, he lay down on the recently fashioned earth and quietly died.

The Invention of Marriage

In addition to creating humans and later saving them from destruction, Nuwa was credited with the invention of marriage. After creating people, the goddess started to travel around the vast and picturesque continents of the newly formed earth. During that journey, she happened upon some of the small clay humans she had made a while before. Unlike most members of that race, the ones Nuwa found seemed sluggish and sick and even had trouble breathing. Also, their skin was wrinkled and their hair was gray. At that moment, the goddess realized that she was witnessing the effects of old age. That made sense because, unlike her, the humans she had fashioned were mortal. Clearly, she would need to make more humans to replace the dying ones. But that would take a lot of time and energy. Then Nuwa had a brilliant idea. If these little beings had the ability to reproduce, *they* could replace *themselves*. So she instituted the concepts of marriage and reproduction through sexual relations. Thereafter, she never again had to create new humans from scratch.

Even in that great god's passing, however, his powers of creation were not yet quelled. Mere seconds after he closed his eyes for the last time, the Shen Yun myth teller says, a miraculous transformation occurred.

His final breath turned into winds and clouds; his voice into rumbling thunder; his left eye blazed into the sun and his right eye gleamed into the moon; his hair and beard became the stars of the Milky Way; his limbs and hands and feet transformed into great mountains and the blood running through his veins into flowing rivers; his flesh converted into fertile farmlands, his bones turned to precious gems and minerals; his teeth and nails became lustrous metals; the hairs on his skin burgeoned into lush vegetation; and the sweat from his extended labors fell as rainwater for the mortal world. . . . Now the skies are graced with luminous celestial bodies, the earth, contoured by great mountains and rivers and flora and fauna galore. And Pan Gu, the giant-god who came out of an egg, is nowhere, yet everywhere to be found.[36]

Humanity's Mighty Mom

The many wondrous natural processes that formed Pangu's final transformation did not happen overnight. Rather, their completion took many thousands of years. In the meantime, a different kind of creation occurred simultaneously, one that was destined to produce large numbers of intelligent beings, some of them divine and others mortal. That second round of creation started in the sky. There, in ways that no one today can explain, large numbers of deities sprang into existence. Only a few of them included Xihe, the sun god; Chang'e, the goddess of the moon; Long Wang, lord of the seas; Caishen, overseer of wealth; XieZhi, god of justice; and Yan Wang, the deity of death.

Long Wang

Also known as the Dragon King, he was the god of the seas and bringer of rain

A Chinese painting from the early 1920s depicts the mother goddess Nuwa, credited with fashioning the human race. The goddess is shown with a human upper half and a snakelike lower half.

These and the other emerging divinities peered down upon the earth and expressed both amazement and admiration for the marvels that Pangu had recently wrought. Nonetheless, one of the newly formed deities sensed that something was missing. Her name was Nuwa, and she had the upper body of a well-proportioned human woman, whereas her lower torso took the form of a dragon's scaly tail and clawed feet. In her view, what the earth lacked was a race of mortal creatures who would give the beautiful but barren world a definite sense of purpose. In addition, she felt, some of those beings might become her friends. After all, the other gods were always busy with their individual personal duties and projects and rarely had time to visit and converse with her.

The goddess decided to make the mortals' top half look like her own. But for reasons that are unclear, she rejected the notion of giving their lower half the look of a dragon. That, the story goes, is why people have smooth skin on their legs and no tail. As for what material to use in making the

Nuwa

Humanity's so-called mother, she was the goddess who created the first human beings from Yellow River clay

little creatures, Nuwa chose the nutrient-rich, yellow-colored clay lying in layers along the Yellow River's banks. When she was ready to begin, she dropped down on her knees and, as one modern

The Mythical Creators of Culture

One of the most important aspects of ancient Chinese mythology, which went hand-in-hand with the creation of humanity, was the invention of human culture. Chinese myths credited most aspects of the creation of culture to five legendary rulers who came to be known collectively as the Five August Emperors. The first of those leaders, Huang-di, was said to have reigned some forty-six hundred years ago. Supposedly, he pioneered the development of mathematics and astronomy. Myths said that he also introduced scales of notes for musicians and tinkered together new measuring instruments for architects and builders. The second mythical culture hero was Huang-di's grandson, Zhuanxu, who initiated several religious customs. The third august emperor, Ku, supposedly loved music so much that he invented several new musical instruments. Ku also commissioned musicians to compose numerous new musical works that thereafter were traditional favorites in China. Ku's son, Yao, the fourth culture hero, was a political genius who united the diverse and often warring Chinese clans, an achievement that made China peaceful and prosperous. The last august emperor, Shun, was said to have instilled in people of all walks of life feelings of shared community spirit. As a result, the Chinese learned to work together and build a better society.

Chinese myth teller writes, scooped up some of the clay and began molding tiny figures having two arms and two legs. "One by one the bitty bods rose up and danced. However, this task soon proved too slow and laborious for the goddess's ambitions. She plucked a branch off a nearby willow, and with a dip and a swish, cast out countless silty splatters. As the droplets landed, each morphed into a little person that instantly pulsed to life."[37]

Humanity on the Brink of Doom

A number of ancient Chinese myths claim that Nuwa did more than create human beings. In addition, she was said to have saved them from utter annihilation a few generations after she brought them into existence. The events leading up to that fateful occasion began when Yan-di, the deity in charge of fire, became irritated with

Gong-gong, god of water. None of the surviving myths that tell the story say exactly why Yan-di was so upset and why he eventually assaulted Gong-gong. What is certain is that the two got into a violent brawl that shook the earth's surface like an earthquake.

Gong-gong lost the fight, and had he retired quietly to find a place to recover, a major crisis might have been averted. However, Gong-gong was so upset that his fellow god had bested him that he threw a tantrum. In a blind rage, he crashed his full weight against the mythical peak of Mount Buzhou, one of the primary pillars installed by Pangu to hold up the heavens. Not surprisingly, the mountain shuddered and the sky started to sag. Soon, writes the Shen Yun myth teller,

> raging fires, devastating floodwaters, and terrifying beasts plagued her realms. The four pillars supporting the heavens crumbled. The sky ruptured. The land cleaved. The planet itself began keeling southeast. Legend says this caused the Earth's axial tilt, celestial bodies' northwest-bound orbits, China's landscape to be higher in the western regions, and most of its rivers to flow toward the southeast.[38]

All this commotion caused earthquakes, forest fires, and floods, each of which killed large numbers of people. Fear and misery spread far and wide, and it appeared to many that humanity might be doomed. Nuwa saw what was happening and decided she must intervene in an effort to save the mortal beings she had fashioned not all that long before. Hurrying to the earth's surface, she located the body of a gigantic turtle that had recently died and used an ax to cut off its legs; she used these to hold up the parts of the sky that had been slumping increasingly downward. Nuwa also saw that holes had formed in the sky. To patch them, she gathered thousands of colored stones and melted them until they formed a puttylike substance. In these ways she rescued humanity from the brink and thereby made all future generations of people possible.

SOURCE NOTES

Introduction: From the Dark Depths: A Burst of Light

1. Quoted in Josephine Mayer and Tom Prideaux, eds., *Never to Die: The Egyptians in Their Own Words*. New York: Viking, 1938, pp. 24–25.
2. Quoted in Mayer and Prideaux, *Never to Die*, p. 25.
3. Robert Carneiro, "Origin Myths," National Center for Science Education, November 3, 2008. https://ncse.ngo.
4. H.W.F. Saggs. *Babylonians*. Berkeley: University of California Press, 2000, p. 32.

Chapter One: The Creation According to the Greeks

5. Edith Hamilton, *Mythology*. New York: Grand Central, 1999, p. 24.
6. W.H.D. Rouse, *Gods, Heroes and Men of Ancient Greece*. New York: New American Library, 2001, p. 11.
7. Ovid, *Metamorphoses*, trans. Horace Gregory. New York: New American Library, 1958, p. 31.
8. Ovid, *Metamorphoses*, pp. 31–32.
9. Quoted in Hamilton, *Mythology*, p. 64.
10. Quoted in Theoi Greek Mythology, "Typhoeus." www.theoi.com.
11. Hesiod, *Theogony*, in *Hesiod, The Homeric Hymns, and Homerica*, trans. H.G. Evelyn-White. Cambridge, MA: Harvard University Press, 1964, p. 135.

Chapter Two: The Creation According to the Babylonians

12. Samuel N. Kramer. *Cradle of Civilization*. New York: Time-Life, 1978, p. 99.
13. Jennifer Westwood. *Gilgamesh and Other Babylonian Tales*. New York: Coward-McCann, 1970, p. 10.
14. W.G. Lambert, trans., *Enuma Elish*, World History Encyclopedia, 2018. www.worldhistory.org.
15. Lambert, *Enuma Elish*.
16. Lambert, *Enuma Elish*.
17. Lambert, *Enuma Elish*.

18. Lambert, *Enuma Elish*.
19. Lambert, *Enuma Elish*.
20. Lambert, *Enuma Elish*.
21. Lambert, *Enuma Elish*.
22. Kramer, *Cradle of Civilization*, pp. 104–106.
23. H.W.F. Saggs, *Civilization Before Greece and Rome*. New Haven, CT: Yale University Press, 1989, p. 293.

Chapter Three: The Creation According to the Aztecs

24. Manuel Aguilar-Moreno, *Handbook to Life in the Aztec World*. New York: Oxford University Press, 2006, p. 139.
25. Quoted in Miguel Leon-Portilla, *Aztec Thought and Culture: A Study of the Ancient Nahuatl Mind*. Norman: University of Oklahoma Press, 1990, p. 90.
26. Leon-Portilla, *Aztec Thought and Culture*, p. 36.
27. Quoted in Fray Bernardino de Sahagun, *Florentine Codex: General History of the Things of New Spain*, vol. 7, trans. Arthur O. Anderson and Charles E. Dibble. Salt Lake City: University of Utah Press, 1950–1969, p. 4.
28. Michael E. Smith, *The Aztecs*. Oxford, England: Blackwell, 2002, p. 208.

Chapter Four: The Creation According to the Hindus

29. Quoted in Monks of Kauai's Hindu Monastery, "Four Facts of Hinduism," 2019. www.himalayanacademy.com.
30. Donna Rosenberg, "The Creation, Death, and Rebirth of the Universe (Hindu Creation Myth)," Genius, 2021. https://genius.com.
31. Mark Cartwright, "Brahma," World History Encyclopedia, 2015. www.ancient.eu.
32. Quoted in Shahrukh Husain, *Demons, Gods, and Holy Men from Indian Myths and Legends*. New York: Peter Bedrick, 1987, p. 59.
33. Kant Singh, trans., "Nasadya Sukta," Academia. www.academia.edu.

Chapter Five: The Creation According to the Chinese

34. Lihui Yang et al., *Handbook of Chinese Mythology*. New York: Oxford University Press, 2005, p. 69.
35. Shen Yun Performing Arts, "Mythhistory Begins," 2016. www.shenyunperformingarts.org.
36. Shen Yun Performing Arts, "Mythhistory Begins."
37. Shen Yun Performing Arts, "Mighty Mom of Mythhistory," 2017. www.shenyunperformingarts.org.
38. Shen Yun Performing Arts, "Mighty Mom of Mythhistory."

FOR FURTHER RESEARCH

Books

Matt Clayton, *Hindu Mythology*. Charleston, SC: Amazon Digital Services, 2018.

Paul Collins, *The Sumerians*. London: Reaktion, 2021.

Tammy Gagne, *Chinese Gods, Heroes, and Mythology*. Minneapolis, MN: ABDO, 2019.

Don Nardo, *Gods of World Mythology*. San Diego, CA: ReferencePoint, 2022.

Katerina Servi, *Greek Mythology: Gods & Heroes; The Trojan War and The Odyssey*. Baton Rouge, LA: Third Millennium, 2018.

David Stuttard, *Roman Mythology: A Traveler's Guide from Troy to Tivoli*. London: Thames and Hudson, 2019.

Isabel Wyatt, *Norse Myths and Viking Legends*. Edinburgh, Scotland: Floris, 2020.

Internet Sources

Subhamoy Das, "10 of the Most Important Hindu Gods," ThoughtCo, 2019. www.thoughtco.com.

Ducksters, "Ancient China: Mythology," 2019. www.ducksters.com.

Hinduwebsite.com, "Brahman: The Supreme Self," 2019. www.hinduwebsite.com.

Katja Mamacos, "Greek Mythology: Olympian Gods and Creation Myths," Travel n History, 2021. https://travelnhistory.com.

Emily Mark, "Most Popular Gods and Goddesses of Ancient China," World History Encyclopedia, 2016. www.ancient.eu.

Donald L. Wasson, "Roman Mythology," World History Encyclopedia, 2018. www.ancient.eu.

Kuan L. Yong, "108 Chinese Mythological Gods and Characters to Know About," Owlcation, 2019. https://owlcation.com.

Websites

Aztec Gods—Who's Who?, Aztec History
www.aztec-history.com/aztec-gods.html
Here, Mexican researcher Jamie Cottrill gives colorfully illustrated summaries of five of the major Aztec gods.

Egyptian Mythology, Tour Egypt
www.touregypt.net/gods1.htm
This helpful general introduction to Egyptian mythology identifies the major kinds of myths and the leading characters in those stories.

The Gods of Chinese Mythology, Godchecker
www.godchecker.com/chinese-mythology/
Conceived by the late modern mythologist Chas Saunders, this informational site explains the best-known ancient Chinese gods in a well-designed, eye-catching format.

Hinduism, History.com
www.history.com/topics/religion/hinduism#section_3
One of the two or three best overall websites on the internet about Hinduism, this offers the basic facts behind Hindu gods, beliefs, sacred writings, rituals, and much more.

Theoi Greek Mythology
www.theoi.com
This is the most comprehensive and reliable general website about Greek mythology on the internet. It features hundreds of separate pages filled with detailed, accurate information, as well as numerous primary sources and reproductions of ancient paintings and mosaics.

INDEX